MW01538304

COPYRIGHT NOTICE

Copyright © 2023, Brandon Witcher

All Rights Reserved.

No part of this ebook may be reproduced, transmitted, downloaded, distributed, stored in any retrieval system, or transmitted in any form or by any means, electronic, mechanical, photocopying, recording, or otherwise, without the prior written permission of the copyright owner, except fair use permitted by copyright law.

Unauthorized copying, sharing, or distribution of this ebook, in whole or in part, is strictly prohibited and is a violation of the copyright holder's rights.

All trademarks, service marks, trade names, and logos appearing in this ebook are the property of their respective owners.

Any unauthorized use of such trademarks, service marks, trade names, or logos is strictly prohibited.

This ebook is licensed for personal use only and may not be distributed or resold without the explicit written permission of the copyright holder.

ADVISORY IS...

ADVISORY IS....
BRANDON WITCHER

CONTENTS

ADVISORY IS...

WHAT IS ADVISORY?

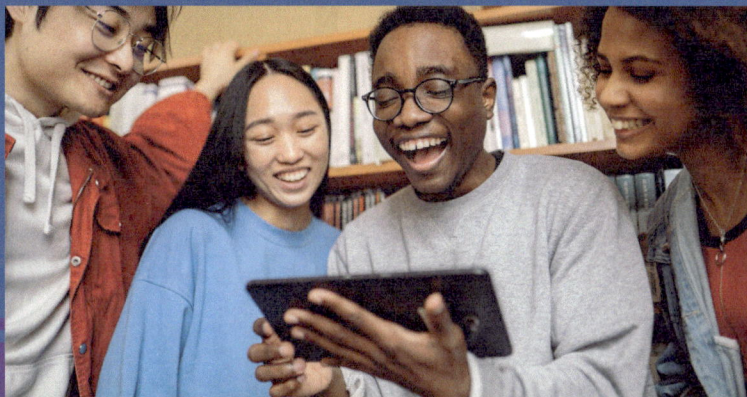

Every human that has reached puberty can confess that middle school and high school are times of difficult transitions. New academic challenges, pressures from society, and hormonal changes can leave young people feeling overwhelmed and disconnected. That's where advisory comes in.

In advisory an environment is created where students are supported and guided through the process of relationship building, increasing their social-emotional capacity, and receiving guidance on their academic progress. Typically, it involves a small group of students (usually around 15-20) meeting regularly with a faculty member or counselor. Most importantly, advisory is a time where young people can connect with their peers and a trusted adult. Advisory programs look vastly different from school to school. Some focus on community or team building activities while others lean more toward academic support, goal-setting, and coaching. The length of advisory can look like an additional 20 minutes of homeroom to a yearlong class with curriculum, assessments, and grades.

Whatever the format, advisory is a critical part of the adolescent experience. It helps students develop a sense of belonging and connection to their school community. It also provides an opportunity for students to receive personalized support and guidance from an adult mentor who knows them well.

We will explore various components of an effective advisory such as how to create a positive and welcoming environment and the fundamentals of an advisory curriculum. Next, we will unpack what happens during advisory and how to support students with academics and social emotional growth. Finally, we will discuss ways to activate family/community stakeholders and setting yourself up for continuous success through reflection and improvement.

Every school, classroom, and student is different. This is not a one size fits all approach. The goal of this workbook is to present best practices of what I have seen as a coach and practitioner. Feel free to take what you need and leave what you don't! With intentional planning and care, your students will be rewarded with a rich experience. So you may have the lingering question, What is advisory?

Advisory is what you make it and step one in making it impactful for both you and your students begins with putting in the work. Let's begin!

Chapter
ONE

ADVISORY IS RESPONSIBILITY

UNDERSTANDING THE ROLE OF AN ADVISOR

Among the many hats that advisors can wear, one is solely dedicated to students developing social and emotional intelligence. Advisors counsel students by building their social skills to navigate the complex dynamics of middle and high school. In a time where screens are ubiquitous and coloring our social interactions, it is imperative to provide young people with the opportunities to unpack these interactions.

Moreover, advisory gives students an opportunity to practice these skills in a safe space. Advisors monitor the growth of students as they learn self management, self-awareness, social awareness, relationship building, and responsible decision making--competencies developed by the Collaborative for Academic and Social Emotional Learning (CASEL Framework).

GREAT ADVISORS CAN BE SEEN:

- Helping students' understand their emotional well being
- Explicitly teaching and modeling social and emotional learning
- Engaging students in discussions around character building
- Supporting students with conflict resolution
- Empowering students to develop their identities and speak their truth
- Building meaningful relationships with students
- Creating opportunities for students to build relationships with one another
- Guiding students as they process challenging emotions and decisions

AN ADVISOR IS A GUIDANCE COUNSELOR

The Role of an Advisor

AN ADVISOR IS A FACILITATOR

The Role of an Advisor

Advisors are educators through and through; not in the traditional sense of lecturing with a blackboard and chalk but as a facilitator of learning. Most of the learning that occurs in advisory is experiential and discussion based. It is incumbent on an advisor to learn discussion and questioning techniques and how to debrief the unique style of learning that happens.

Additionally, advisors monitor their students' grades, attendance, and overall academic progress. By facilitating conversations, students can make informed choices about this data by creating action plans to address gaps. Moreover, an important function of the advisor is to help students with setting realistic and attainable goals, both academic and personal. Advisors may also provide tutoring or refer students to academic support services.

GREAT ADVISORS CAN BE SEEN:

- Facilitating team building activities
- Engaging students in journaling
- Debriefing students to help them understand the purpose of advisory activities
- Conferring with students about their academic progress
- Helping students calendar and get organized
- Tutoring students to support academic skill development
- Modeling for students how to create SMART goals and develop action plans for success

One of the most gratifying roles of an advisor is to serve as a connector. Advisors become a liaison between students, families, the school, and the community. They provide updates on student progress and address any concerns or questions that families may have. They know the student well and can speak to families with specific knowledge and examples of how the student is doing in school.

Advisors act as a bridge between the community and the school. This sounds a bit daunting but could be as simple as facilitating a field trip or bringing in a guest speaker. For advisory to work at its apex, all stakeholders must be involved. The advisor holds the key to bridging the gap and using the power of the community to influence a young person's life.

AN ADVISOR IS A LIFE COACH
The Role of an Advisor

Advisors assist students with the transition from middle school to high school and from high school to life. Both of these are critical times in human psychological development and without guidance many students are lost, left to figure things out on their own. Advisors can step in and support students as they uncover their life's passion. This by no means is an easy task and takes a lot of practice and guidance. Advisors are essential in helping students to make a plan for their future and preparing them to embark on that journey.

GREAT ADVISORS CAN BE SEEN:

- Conferencing with young people and their families about grades, attendance, and positive/negative interactions in school
- Addressing families' concerns or questions and keeping them aware of school events
- Connecting students with community service opportunities
- Leveraging community stakeholders to support learning
- Recommending students for clubs, jobs, or programs that are available in the community
- Coordinating guest speakers to share real world experiences

GREAT ADVISORS CAN BE SEEN:

- Consulting on high school/college course selection, college admission requirements, and career opportunities
- Exposing students to broad experiences to expand their world view
- Planning and road mapping with students to document post graduation plans
- Discussing and offering experiential/hands-on opportunities for students to engage in their passions/interests
- Exploring high school/college/career options with students
- Highlighting skills and competencies that will help students to be successful in their chosen high school/college/career pathways
- Supporting students as they develop interest based projects

AN ADVISOR IS A CONNECTOR
The Role of an Advisor

Chapter TWO

ADVISORY IS HOME

CREATING AN ENVIRONMENT OF CARE, SAFETY, AND RESPECT

PHYSICAL ENVIRONMENT

Most advisories take place in classrooms. Depending on funding or your artistic expertise, it may still look like a classroom. By thinking about the physical space, you can maximize students' comfort level and, with the right design, make students forget that this is also where they have Algebra class! Consider the following questions as you design the physical layout of your space.

What is on the walls?

Pictures or decor that represent your students and their interests make them feel at home. Student-created vision boards or family photos add a nice personal touch. Don't forget to add items that represent you. Hang photos from trips abroad or your college diploma. Maybe include pictures of some of your hobbies that students don't know about. Be sure that your co-created advisory norms are posted for reference. An agenda for the time in advisory should also be posted. Additionally, give your advisory its own space or bulletin board to post projects, celebrations or other advisory happenings.

How is furniture arranged?

School desks have come a long way since the rows of hard plastic chairs attached to wooden planks by metal bars. There are multiple options for school furniture that allow for maximum collaboration and group work that would be great to use during advisory. But if you are having a circle discussion, can desks be arranged in a way that no one is hidden? Can the room be segmented to give you privacy to work with a student one on one while everyone else is independently working? If allowed, think about adding some other homey touches like a lamp or a rug. These might seem unnecessary but they go a long way in making students feel at home.

PHYSICAL ENVIRONMENT

Creating an environment that promotes safety and respect will enable students to feel comfortable enough to share their thoughts, feelings, and concerns. This starts with the physical space.

How is the classroom organized?

Think about what is going to happen during your advisory time. What routines/procedures do you have in place to distribute & collect things? If you have a short amount of time for advisory this is extremely important. You don't want to take five minutes to pass out student journals if your advisory period is only thirty minutes. Post a daily agenda in a familiar place so students can see what they will be doing in advisory. Think about student groupings. Remember, advisory is a time for students to get to know one another. Assigned seats ensure students can interact with people other than their friends. Lastly, consider procedures for independent student work and one on one conversations. Having these organized will make the time you have in advisory much more efficient.

What are your entrance/exit routines?

Young people are creatures of habit and usually thrive when they know exactly what to do. What will students do as they enter the advisory space? Will this happen everyday or will there be a weekly schedule to follow?

When students enter the classroom/advisory space greet them at the door. This helps to transition them into the space and prepare for the learning that will take place. This also gives you an opportunity to do quick check-ins with students and assess where they are before beginning the advisory activity.

SOCIAL & EMOTIONAL ENVIRONMENT

Now that your advisory space LOOKS the part, it's time to make it FEEL like an advisory space.

For advisory to function at its highest level, students must have a feeling of safety and respect. When students feel safe, they are more likely to take risks, explore new ideas, and develop meaningful relationships with their peers and teachers. Having respect for others' differences and beliefs is an essential part of creating a safe and supportive community. This section will discuss several strategies to create an environment of safety and respect.

Earning Trust

A positive advisory experience begins with building trust. This is a very difficult and delicate thing to do. However, the quickest way to do it is by moving very slowly. Advisors will need to establish trust with their students by modeling respectful and supportive behaviors, being honest and transparent, and creating space for students to share confidential information.

Respect is often at the top of the list when students discuss teachers they don't like. It is hard to trust someone who doesn't listen or value your opinions. Students are no different. Have conversations and set clear expectations about respect with your advisory. What does respect look like to them? On the converse, what does it look like if someone disrespected them? Chart these findings with students and help them to understand how their families and society have shaped these feelings. Above all, honor their feelings and experiences. Ensure advisory expectations and norms are consistently reinforced to maintain a respectful environment.

A huge part of students being able to trust you is knowing that they have been seen and heard. Validate their feelings and experiences often. This stepping stone to trust will encourage students to communicate with their advisors about academic struggles, emotional challenges, and other concerns. There is no way to include all of the methods to gain a students' trust in this book. By taking it one day at a time, being consistent and showing up, you are in it to win it.

When correcting behavior refer to the norms you create. Students should know that the norms are ever present and govern conduct in the advisory space.

Establishing Clear Boundaries

Establishing clear boundaries is another critical component of creating a safe environment. When establishing boundaries there is a simple maxim for students: this is what you are going to do, and this is what you are not going to do. What are your advisory's non-negotiables? Standing firm on issues like "respecting the opinions of others" or "using language to uplift and not demean" will go a long way in guiding students to reciprocate respect for one another and growing as a community, even through disagreements.

Another area to draw clear boundaries is around what is discussed in advisory. By making certain topics of discussion off limits, students can share without the fear of something being repeated or something making them feel uncomfortable. Establishing guidelines and expectations can help students understand what is expected of them and what types of conversation are not acceptable. Additionally, you must communicate to students clearly what these boundaries look like. Be vigilant and monitor conversations to hold everyone accountable. As an activity you might ask students to brainstorm a list of topics that may make others feel uncomfortable. These can be written down and shared with everyone.

As you design your classroom norms be sure that they don't sound like rules. Most rules are meant to be broken. Instead of telling students what not to do, try to focus the language of the expectation on the desirable behavior. For example, "don't take other people's things" could be rewritten as "we respect the possessions and space of our advisory members".

Be the example for your students. Just make sure the example is clear and consistent so it is effective. If there is a non-negotiable rule around using cellphones during circle discussions you might model silencing your own cell phone and putting it on your desk during the circle talk. It is beneficial to involve students in creating these boundaries (in the form of classroom expectations and norms) to foster ownership and responsibility. Check out this lesson that will help guide you and students as you create expectations together.

ADVISORY LESSON PLAN: SETTING EXPECTATIONS

This lesson is great to do on the first day of advisory. This activity could be done during a normal 45 minute period with minimal planning/prep.

PURPOSE

Setting clear expectations helps students understand boundaries and how they should conduct themselves in the advisory. They are the cornerstone to creating an environment of safety and respect for all students.

CASEL Competency/SEL Focus:
Responsible decision making about behaviors that will benefit the class community

MATERIALS

Projector/Whiteboard
Chart Paper
Markers

ACTIVITY

Break students into groups. Inform them that we will be engaging in a very important task, setting expectations. Unlike times before, your advisor isn't just going to give you a list of rules or expectations and expect you to enforce them. The advisory will work together to come up with a list of norms where everyone has input. First, students will discuss in groups what their ideal classroom environment looks like and a group member will capture the conversation. Give students a few prompts to guide the discussion: What is on the walls?, How do students treat one another? How does the teacher treat the students? Next, they will discuss which behaviors, expectations, or rules have to be put into place to make their vision a reality. After about 5-10 mins. (depending on your grade level) have the groups share out. The advisor will chart the responses on the board. Some time can be taken to combine expectations and eliminate ones that are negative or sound like rules (i.e. "Don't do...", You shouldn't...").

Have students go back to their groups and put the list in order of importance. Once again have students share out. Probe them by asking why they put their list in that order. As an advisory come to a consensus on a final list of norms. Assign a student to make a poster with the norms on them to hang in the advisory space. A similar process can be followed to have students create norms for the advisor.

DEBRIEF

- Which one of the expectations is going to be the hardest for you?
- Do you think our norms will need to be changed later in the year? Why?
- Tell me what the process was like to help decide the expectations for the room. How did your group make decisions?
- What are some expectations that you have for me as your advisor?

SOCIAL & EMOTIONAL ENVIRONMENT

Building relationships take time. Be patient with your students and with yourself.

Fostering a Sense of Belonging

Creating a sense of belonging is key to promoting a respectful and inclusive environment where young people feel connected to the school community. By cultivating an environment where students feel valued and heard, advisors become the catalysts to students loving their school. Students will participate more during class, volunteer for school functions, and enjoy their time at school. Advisors can foster a sense of belonging by recognizing each student's unique contributions, creating opportunities for students to work together, and highlighting the importance of a diverse and inclusive community. One of the best ways that a sense of belonging can be cultivated is by giving your advisory an identity. Create an advisory flag, motto, handshake, or mascot. Think about getting a "pet" that stays in the advisory. (My advisory had a pet rock named Boomer). Engage in challenges with other advisories to promote healthy competition. Young people are in desperate need to be accepted by their peers. Involving them as a member of the advisory accomplishes this. After some time many students refer to their advisory as their family.

Creating an environment of safety and respect is a crucial part of a successful advisory program. By fostering trust, setting clear boundaries, and fostering a sense of belonging, students are more likely to feel connected, respected, and supported. An advisory class that prioritizes creating a safe space can have a long-lasting impact on students' academic success and social-emotional development.

WHERE DO I START?

Use these tips to get started with creating a space that is safe and respectful for all

1. Set clear expectations for behavior, language, and communication. Take time to review acceptable behaviors with students to be sure they are clear about what these expectations look like.
2. Encourage students to reflect on their personal beliefs about respect and be sure to communicate them with one another. Build in systems that encourage active reflection and support for students having difficulty expressing themselves.
3. Use diverse teaching strategies that allow students to participate, learn, and succeed. Additionally, utilize activities that appeal to multiple intelligences and are fun.
4. Educate yourself: Learn about different cultures, traditions, and norms to be more understanding and accepting of your students. Take the time to learn about the cultures and traditions of your advisory. Invite them to share their culture with the class so everyone can learn. Let them be the experts!
5. Create systems for active reflection. When students are triggered or upset what happens? If there is a disagreement, what steps will you take to ensure that it is a teachable moment?

Chapter
THREE

ADVISORY IS LEARNING

DEVELOPING A PLAN FOR ADVISORY

Don't just jump in and start writing your advisory curriculum! Do a little pre planning to help make sure your planning time is focused.

Students' Needs Come First

Before beginning to tackle learning maps or lesson plans, it is imperative to think about students' needs first. Seventh graders will not likely need the same support as high school seniors. Advisors must identify the specific issues and challenges faced by students and tailor the curriculum to address those concerns.

For inspiration, it is a great idea to have a conversation with students. One of the most underutilized resources in curriculum development is student input. Ask students directly what pressing concerns or topics are on their mind or what they are struggling with. You may even give them a survey to offer suggestions in a low risk and confidential manner. Additionally, consider observing students to collect your own anecdotal data. Find out what social and emotional skills are lacking and take the opportunity to develop lessons to address them.

Think of the End First

Advisory curriculum is dynamic and should change to meet the needs of students. But that doesn't mean that there shouldn't be any planning. Weekly, monthly, and quarterly goals will help keep your advisory on track. Before you begin developing activities, think about the end first. If your advisory was wildly successful, what would it look like? Once you have created this vision for success, map it out and work backwards. What would students be doing? Adults? Think about the attitudes and behaviors you would like for students to take into the real world with them. These should help focus your curricular planning. Additionally, consider the school and district vision for students. How can you incorporate these to help develop students' skills to make these visions a success?

SOCIAL EMOTIONAL LEARNING

RESOURCE GUIDE

Since advisory aims to support students' social and emotional development, SEL MUST be integrated into the curriculum. Integrating SEL into your curriculum can be a bit of a challenge at first. You may be thinking, how do I teach a student skills like perseverance and leadership? Where are the curricular products that support self-awareness? You have to approach SEL like it's any other subject matter. Become a student yourself and dive into the material as a learner. These resources can help your self education.

CASEL

The Collaborative for Academic Social and Emotional learning is the leading think tank for all things SEL. They have a wealth of resources and research to support implementation of SEL from the classroom to the district level.

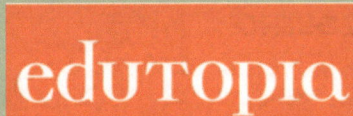

EDUTOPIA

Edutopia.com is a website focused on education innovation, offering resources, research, and strategies for teachers, parents, and administrators to improve student learning experiences.

SECOND STEP

The Second Step website offers research-based programs and resources for SEL and bullying prevention. It focuses on promoting social skills, emotional regulation, and responsible decision-making.

COMMITTEE FOR CHILDREN

The Committee for Children provides information and resources for families, caregivers, and professionals on child and family health and well-being, education, and support services in San Diego County.

HARMONY SEL

The Harmony SEL website provides social and emotional learning resources for educators, parents, and students. It offers practical tools, activities, and strategies to promote positive relationships, resilience, and well-being.

BREAKING DOWN THE

ADVISORY LEARNING MAP

Use this process to guide you or your team through developing an advisory road map or tailoring an SEL curriculum to your needs.

START

1. DEFINE THE PURPOSE AND GOALS OF THE ADVISORY PROGRAM

Before designing the curriculum, clarify the goals and intended outcomes of your program. Do you want to focus on academic support, social-emotional learning, college and career readiness, or a combination of these areas?If advisory is wildly successful, what will students be able to do at the end of the year? Be sure to include any relevant school wide or district wide student facing expectations as you define your purpose and goals.

2. DEVELOP A SCOPE AND SEQUENCE

Outline the topics that will be covered in each grade level or semester. Consider the developmental needs of your students and align the content with your program goals. Develop weekly, monthly, and quarterly goals that align with your vision of a successful student.

3. INCLUDE DIVERSE VOICES, ENGAGING ACTIVITIES, AND TONS OF FUN

In most cases, advisory does not have the same scrutiny as traditional classes. Take this as an opportunity to be creative. Include topics that are relevant and meaningful to your students while engaging in project based learning/experiential learning. Activities should promote student participation, reflection, and collaboration. Advisory activities need to give students an opportunity to critically think and publicly speak about a diverse range of topics. Most of all it should be FUN!

4.SEEK HELP IF YOU NEED IT

There are many individuals with SEL experience that could assist you with the development of curriculum. Speak with veteran teachers, your principal, or a district supervisor to get feedback on your learning map.

READY, SET, LAUNCH!

You are now ready to write amazing advisory lesson plans!

END

START WITH THE END

The key to planning out skills for advisory starts with backward planning. Use this tool to think about what skills, mindsets, and dispositions students will have either at the end of the school year or when they graduate (for multi-year planning).

SEL SKILLS FOR FUTURE SUCCESS

WHEN MY STUDENTS GRADUATE THEY WILL BE ABLE TO........ (ACTIONS)

MINDSETS/VALUES OF STUDENTS WHEN THEY GRADUATE

BEHAVIORS OF STUDENTS WHEN THEY GRADUATE

ACADEMIC SKILLS FOR FUTURE SUCCESS

MONTHLY PLANNER

SKILL FOCUS:

MONTH OF:

INDICATORS OF SUCCESS:

WEEK 1

WEEK 2

WEEK 3

WEEK 4

SKILL FOCUS:

MONTH OF:

INDICATORS OF SUCCESS:

WEEK 1

WEEK 2

WEEK 3

WEEK 4

SKILL FOCUS:

MONTH OF:

INDICATORS OF SUCCESS:

WEEK 1

WEEK 2

WEEK 3

WEEK 4

MONTHLY PLANNER

SKILL FOCUS:

MONTH OF:
_____

INDICATORS OF SUCCESS:
_____
_____
_____
_____
_____

WEEK 1
_____
WEEK 2
_____
WEEK 3
_____
WEEK 4
_____
_____

SKILL FOCUS:

MONTH OF:
_____

INDICATORS OF SUCCESS:
_____
_____
_____
_____
_____

WEEK 1
_____
WEEK 2
_____
WEEK 3
_____
WEEK 4
_____
_____

SKILL FOCUS:

MONTH OF:
_____

INDICATORS OF SUCCESS:
_____
_____
_____
_____
_____

WEEK 1
_____
WEEK 2
_____
WEEK 3
_____
WEEK 4
_____
_____

MONTHLY PLANNER

SKILL FOCUS:

MONTH OF:

INDICATORS OF SUCCESS:

WEEK 1

WEEK 2

WEEK 3

WEEK 4

SKILL FOCUS:

MONTH OF:

INDICATORS OF SUCCESS:

WEEK 1

WEEK 2

WEEK 3

WEEK 4

SKILL FOCUS:

MONTH OF:

INDICATORS OF SUCCESS:

WEEK 1

WEEK 2

WEEK 3

WEEK 4

MONTHLY PLANNER

SKILL FOCUS:

MONTH OF:

INDICATORS OF SUCCESS:

WEEK 1

WEEK 2

WEEK 3

WEEK 4

SKILL FOCUS:

MONTH OF:

INDICATORS OF SUCCESS:

WEEK 1

WEEK 2

WEEK 3

WEEK 4

SKILL FOCUS:

MONTH OF:

INDICATORS OF SUCCESS:

WEEK 1

WEEK 2

WEEK 3

WEEK 4

HOW TO WRITE AN ADVISORY LESSON PLAN

Advisory lesson plans will look different depending on your school's advisory situation. Generally, advisory lesson plans are just like standard lesson plans. Make sure that you are crystal clear about what skills students will be working on during advisory.

PURPOSE/SEL FOCUS

Check your school district's SEL competencies. States are continuing to adopt their own standards for SEL. If your state does not have competencies then you can use the CASEL 5 Framework. These can be broken down into monthly units with weekly focuses. Additionally, you can use your district's SEL resources or other curricular products to supplement your planning.

MATERIALS

Include materials that will be needed for the activity here.

ACTIVITY

Intro/Opening Activity:
This is a great time to have students reflect on where they are emotionally when they come in. The opening sets the tone and will help ground students before the main advisory activity/discussion. Students can journal on a specific topic, have a moment of silent meditation, or even check their grades to prepare for a one on one conference.

Activity/Discussion:
This is where many teachers struggle. Explicitly teaching SEL content doesn't look or feel "natural". There isn't a textbook that demonstrates how to teach self awareness. Those with counseling and psychology backgrounds are a little more prepared but lack the pedagogical understanding educators have. There is a happy medium, but unfortunately it is going to take some time and experimentation to get it right. Activities should be thought provoking and/or fun. Additionally, advisory activities should focus on getting students to know one another. Any activities that have students communicating or moving around is a good start. As your unit progresses, you can focus more on explicitly teaching SEL skills.

DEBRIEF

This is where the learning is processed for the first time. All advisory activities should be thoroughly debriefed to allow students time to take in the new information as well as clarify the learning. Finding time to debrief with students at the end of the lesson helps them see why the skill is important and how it can be used in the real world. Plus, it gives them an opportunity to reflect on their own behaviors during the activity. No matter what, don't skip this step!

ADVISORY LESSON PLANNING

WHERE DO I START?

Start by **taking a look at the monthly/weekly goals for the advisory**. Next, brainstorm bite size skills, behaviors, and/or themes you'd like to target. It could be social-emotional learning skills, building community, or enhancing students' self-confidence in specific areas. Most importantly, think about behaviors you'd like to see in the future. These can be for the entire class or individual students.

Next, consider students' interests: observe and talk to your advisory about hobbies, passions, and talents. This will help you **find activities that are engaging and meaningful to them**. Take the time to understand the dynamics of your advisory. Would they like discussions based on interesting readings or more hands-on group activities? Do they struggle when working in groups or should the activities be individual assignments? Having a healthy mix of activities will both satisfy and challenge students.

Always remember to be inclusive when choosing advisory activities. Take note of the needs and abilities of all the students in the advisory, including those with special needs or specific learning styles. Think about **incorporating activities based on multiple intelligences and ability levels**.

Mix up the types of activities, so they range from group challenges, reflective writing, games, and discussions.

Finally, **seek feedback**. Ask students how the activities went and if they would like to suggest an activity for the following sessions. By inviting students' feedback you are building trust and giving students ownership of what they are learning.

20 Things You Can Do During Advisory

1. Icebreaker games
2. Goal setting for the school year
3. Brainstorming ways to improve the school
4. Learning about study skills and time management
5. Mindfulness activities and meditation
6. Team-building exercises
7. Career/College exploration activities
8. Learning about stress and emotion regulation
9. Circle Talks
10. Conflict resolution and communication skills training
11. Service projects and volunteering
12. Creative writing prompts and journaling
13. Sports and fitness activities
14. Character education lessons
15. Thought-provoking discussions and debates
16. Guest speakers and presentations
17. Interest exploration activities
18. Public speaking & communication skills training
19. Work on a passion project
20. Cultural celebrations and diversity awareness activities

Chapter
FOUR

ADVISORY IS CONNECTION

BUILDING RELATIONSHIPS WITH STUDENTS

BUILDING TRUSTING RELATIONSHIPS

Building relationships with students is definitely an art and not a science. It takes time, patience, and care to build trust with young people

Foundation of Trust

For students to trust you, they must know that you care. Caring relationships are not built overnight and all of them are different, just as the needs of the young people you work with. Intentional time must be invested to slowly build the foundation of trust necessary to have real relationships with students.

Consider investments into a "relationship piggy bank". Every individual conversation, every connection, and interaction you have with a student is a deposit in the relationship piggy bank. When students are misbehaving and feeling dejected, unresponsive, or angry the time for a withdrawal from the bank can occur. Getting that student to trust you and tell you what is wrong in that moment is extremely valuable for the student who is likely still learning to manage emotions. It also is a great tool to leverage for your classroom management practice. Likewise, you can't make a withdrawal from the bank if you don't have any currency in cultivating that relationship. The trust and rapport you have will let the student know that you see them beyond a singular moment in their life and that you aren't defining them because of it. Consider the following ways essential in building trust with students.

Show Empathy

Building positive relationships starts with understanding the students' experiences, challenges, and interests. Kids come to school with all kinds of baggage. They have faced challenges that may be beyond the parameters of your own understanding and experience. Show empathy by listening actively to their concerns, acknowledging their emotions, and trying to see things from their perspective. Seek to understand without judgment and, if necessary, connect them with resources to support.

Communicate Effectively

Effective communication is essential for building positive relationships with students. Be clear and concise with instructions, listen actively, and provide constructive feedback that is specific and actionable. Encourage students to communicate their thoughts and feelings and provide opportunities for dialogue and discussion.

BUILDING TRUSTING RELATIONSHIPS

Building relationships with students is definitely an art and not a science. It takes time, patience, and care to build trust with young people.

Show Interest in Their Lives

It is super easy to find common ground with students. By simply asking them what foods they enjoy or what shows they have been binge watching recently, the door can open to a really great conversation. Acknowledge important events and milestones (birthdays, awards, etc.) in their lives by showing your support and encouragement. This could extend beyond the classroom as well. Take time to attend school supported functions such as sports games or concerts. Congratulate them for a job well done and just watch their faces light up.

Be Consistent and Reliable

Building positive relationships requires you to be consistent and reliable. Consistency with your expectations is key. Students will often test boundaries and being inconsistent can be easily spotted among students. A few will even find opportunities to take advantage of these inconsistent expectations. Often, mixed messages can be confusing and have students feeling singled out and targeted. Make sure that you are giving constant feedback and following through on your promises and commitments, especially rewards and consequences. Students will know they can rely on you and will seek out your help.

Forgive

Forgiveness is a powerful tool in helping to establish trust early on. Students are going to do things that upset you, that is a given. In establishing relationships, we can't carry the negative emotions associated with their behavior. At times this can be a tall order, but it is necessary to forgive. Forgiving young people helps us release negativity that can linger and make us biased, affecting the relationship with the student moving forward. Forgiveness is also a form of self care that helps you to show up as your best self despite the myriad challenges.

Celebrate Successes

Celebrating small successes and achievements help teens build confidence and self-esteem. It strengthens their relationships with you. Recognize and praise students for their efforts, progress, and achievements. Moreover, there should be a space and time for students to share their success with their advisory. Below is an activity you can do with your advisory to celebrate one another.

ADVISORY LESSON PLAN: AWARDS CEREMONY

This lesson is great to do near the end of a marking period. This activity has flexible timing (between 20–50 mins) with minimal planning/prep.

PURPOSE

Students aren't often celebrated by one another. This activity allows students to honor their peers creatively. This is also a great way for students to recognize the growth they have seen in one another.

CASEL Competency/SEL Focus:
Building Social Awareness by recognizing the strengths in others and expressing gratitude

MATERIALS

Projector/Whiteboard
White Paper Plates
Colored pencils/Markers

ACTIVITY

Have students answer a journal prompt to open the activity. Prompt: Make a list of your accomplishments this past marking period, both inside and outside of school. Some students may struggle to think of an accomplishment. You may add some examples on the board to give them ideas. Advisor will pair students up and they will share their accomplishments with their partner. The partner will take one of these accomplishments and create an award. He/she/they will decorate the paper plate like a certificate including the student's name and accomplishment. Give students time to be creative and decorate their awards.

Next, students will take turns presenting the awards in front of the advisory. You can even have the winner come up and give an acceptance speech thanking those who helped make the accomplishment possible if time permits. To scaffold this activity you can write suggestions of awards that can be given out and post it for inspiration. These don't have to be just academic in nature: consider awards for Best School Spirit, Great Friend, or Super Helpful.

DEBRIEF

- How did it feel to be celebrated?
- What award are you most proud of receiving? Why?
- Why is it important to celebrate one another?
- Fill in the blank: I'd like to express gratitude to _____ for helping me with _____.

QUESTIONS TO CONNECT WITH KIDS

1 WHAT'S SOMETHING I NEED TO KNOW ABOUT YOU?

2 WHAT WAS THE LAST THING YOU GOOGLED?

3 WHAT ARE YOU BINGE WATCHING?

4 TELL ME HOW SCHOOL IS GOING.

5 WHAT'S SOMETHING THAT YOU ARE GOOD AT?

6 WHAT GAMES ARE YOU PLAYING?

7 WHAT IS SOMETHING THAT YOU WOULD CHANGE ABOUT OUR SCHOOL?

CIRCLE TALKS

Of all the evidence based practices for advisory, none have as much impact as Circle Talks. This practice inherently improves communication skills, empathy, and understanding of diverse perspectives.

Basically, a circle talk is a structured conversation that gives everyone an opportunity to speak and to be heard by everyone else in the advisory. Research suggests that incorporating circle talks as an ongoing practice has shown significant improvement in communication, social interaction, and resiliency. Circle talks are a great tool for promoting equality, active listening, and inclusivity. At the outset this practice may seem very simple; however, there are a lot of nuances to consider for circle talks to be effective.

Before beginning a circle talk the physical space needs to be adjusted. Chairs and tables should be positioned so that everyone that is participating in the circle has an unobstructed view of everyone else. Usually this looks like everyone sitting in a chair in a circle with nothing in the middle to block someone's view. Music may be played to set the mood but when sharing begins it should be turned off to allow everyone a fair opportunity to be heard.

AS YOU DEVELOP YOUR CIRCLE NORMS, CONSIDER THE FOLLOWING:

There needs to be some preparation before your circle talk. First, very clear expectations need to be developed. These expectations aid participants in enacting the values of circle talks—equity, active listening, and inclusivity. These norms should mimic but be separate from advisory norms.

- What kinds of behavior would I like to see?
- What expectations can I include about equity of voice?
- What expectations can I include that will help students be respectful?
- Are there expectations for having disagreements or respectfully disagreeing?
- Should there be an expectation for participation in the circle talk?
- What can I say to remind students to be honest, kind, engaged, etc.?

Here are a few examples of expectations:
1. Circle is not a time for a debate, everyone is entitled to their own opinion without judgment.
2. Lean into the discomfort.
3. Everyone speaks once before anyone can speak a second time.
4. Thinking time is time to come up with my response, speaking time is time for me to listen to others.
5. Use kind words, always.
6. We assume that everyone is speaking from a good heart and has good intentions.
7. If you need some time away from the talk, raise your hand to be excused.
8. Our circle talks are confidential; what happens in circle, stays in circle.

Circle Talks take practice to get right. Be committed and see it through. They get better each time you do them.

Preparing for Circle

Next, you are ready to choose topics for your circle talk. Topics should be formatted as open ended questions. You may also consider having students complete a required reading or viewing to support the discussion. Topics should be broad and correlate with your school's mission and vision for students, current SEL curriculum, or based on an observational need. For example, if you notice that five of your students quit their after school activity you may want to discuss perseverance and how people make decisions on when to call it quits or when to stick it out. Depending on how much time you have allotted, you may need to have a few follow up questions prepared.

Time to Circle Up

Once all of these measures are put into place it is time to circle up! One of the ways to ensure equity of voice is to use a talking piece. This item is only held by the person speaking with everyone else listening. Most circles begin with the facilitator giving a little background on the discussion topic, asking the first prompt, and then passing the talking stick to his/her/their right or left. Each person takes a turn answering the prompt until the talking piece arrives back to the facilitator.

After all questions have been presented and the piece arrives back to the facilitator he/she/they find a way to close the circle. Usually this is by using a quote or leaving a minute or two of silent reflection for everyone to process. This is totally up to you and as you continue to refine your circle practices it will become second nature. Try not to force anything. If it doesn't feel right, try a different approach the next time.

Potential Issues

Potential issues that may arise during circle talks are easy to spot and take redirection, reinforcement of norms, and consistency to overcome. The most common issue is a student not wanting to participate or share. This is likely a multitiered problem but for the context of circle talks, the goal is to get the young person to say something, even if it's just their name or answer yes or no, or even repeat what someone else has said. More adolescents are finding it difficult to speak in public or honestly share their opinions with their peers. By getting him/her/them to participate, even on a minor level, it accomplishes two things: 1. Building trust with the student so they share when they are ready and 2. Promoting an environment of safety by allowing the student to slowly take on the risk of sharing with others.

CIRCLE TALKS

There is no perfect way to do circle talks. When you find what works for your advisory, you won't be able to get your young people to stop sharing.
(a very good problem to have!)

Potential Issues cont'd

The second common issue is students monopolizing the sharing time with the talking piece. If this happens gently remind students that everyone needs an opportunity to share. You may also use a nonverbal signal to let the speaker know it is time to wrap up their thoughts and pass the talking piece to the next person. Another common occurrence is students not sharing their true feelings or sharing with reservations. This often takes time to overcome. Students MUST FEEL SAFE when sharing with their peers. The best way to guide them over this hump is to begin circle talks with very low risk questions/prompts.

Low-risk Circle Talk Prompts

1. What superhero is most like you personally? In what ways?
2. Think about the best meal/food you've ever had in your life. What was it and what made it the best meal of your life?
3. Think about all of the years you have spent in school. What is your best memory of school?
4. What makes a good friend? Are you a good friend? Why or why not?
5. What are three things that really grind your gears?

These prompts are accessible and still give everyone some insight into the world of the speaker. Continue to reinforce norms and gently redirect to make sure students continue to be honest in the circle talk interactions.

Overall, circle talks foster deeper connections and understanding between teens and teachers, by building a positive advisory culture. Follow these steps and you will be on a path to start a safe, encouraging, and meaningful circle talk practice with your advisory.

WHERE DO I START?

Use these tips to get started with your first Circle Talk

1. Set clear expectations for behavior, and communication in circle. Be sure students are clear about what these behaviors look like. Share norms and hold students accountable for upholding them.
2. Look up circle facilitation advice online. Find 1-2 practices to try during your first circle talk.
3. Write out a Circle Talk agenda and practice facilitating with colleagues at a team meeting.
4. Decide on a talking piece and question prompts. They should be low risk and easy to answer.
5. Arrange the room so that each person has an unobstructed view of everyone else.

DEALING WITH DIFFICULT STUDENTS

When you are facing young people who are having difficulties with advisory there is usually a deeper reason they are struggling that needs to be uncovered.

Be Patient

Advisory is usually a new experience for many students. After reinforcing norms and expectations, there may be a few students that just aren't bought-in to making the advisory culture the best it could be. Be patient with these students. Their disengagement, defiance, or avoidance is a way to communicate with you. What follows is a list of strategies you can use to deal with students who are struggling to connect.

Daily Checkins

Students who are difficult usually demand a lot of attention. Checking-in with them daily can alert you to potential problems or disruptions to advisory well in advance of the disruptive behavior. One rule that works is to have an expectation that students tell you if they are not having a good day. Students will be forthright and potentially avoid an escalated situation because you will be more aware and careful to maintain a supportive and caring environment for all.

Listen Actively and Validate Their Feelings

Before misbehavior/disengagement becomes an issue, try to get them to be open to just the idea of having a dialogue first. Prompt them with a question then just listen. Take the time to repeat back what students are saying to you. Help them clarify and pinpoint their sources of frustrations to come to a solution that can work for everyone. Many students get angry at adults in school simply because they feel they are not being heard. Take the time to listen to students, even when they don't think you are listening. Let them know that you understand their feelings and empathize with their situation. If listening in the moment is a challenge, consider having students write out what they'd like to communicate first then review the statement with the student.

Remain Calm

Students who don't participate or consistently misbehave can transfer feelings of frustration and anger to the adult. It is important that you keep your cool and demonstrate the behavior that you would like for your advisory to have. Students have difficulty regulating their own emotions. Remaining calm models that you are in full control of your emotions, regardless of outside influences. When speaking with a student who is being disrespectful, take a deep breath and just remember there is a reason for this behavior.

Be aware of your responses to negative student behaviors. They are clues to how you process and respond to your own trauma.

Avoid Judging and Interrupting

All students should have the opportunity to explain themselves, whether they are right or wrong. It is a great way to teach them self awareness and self reflection in the moment. It is imperative to be an observer when students are given the difficult task of reflecting on their behavior. It is easy to make snap judgments, revert to sarcasm, or interrupt students attempting to explain what happened. This can be really damaging to your relationship with that student and may diminish trust and increase resentment. Remember to actively listen and stay calm. Judging and interrupting are both reactions fueled by your own emotions and ego. It is necessary for you to be in control of your emotions to help students manage theirs.

Seek to Understand, then Heal the Harm

When a student is misbehaving or completely disengaged, seek to understand the behavior first. More often than not the student is trying to communicate some difficulty they may be having but don't have the words to verbalize it. As educators attempting to build relationships and gain your students' trust you have to do the work to understand the behavior first. Only then can you process the events with the young person. During this time, expectations should be reinforced and retaught if necessary. Also, the student should think about how to restore the hurt or harm that was caused by his/her/their behavior. This could look like an apology (written or said aloud), community service, or an agreed upon solution of your design. It goes without saying that the student must be at the center of the act that restores the harm caused by his/her/their behavior.

Follow Up With Praise

If a kid has a rough day in advisory, be sure to follow up with them. It is a great way to let them know that you care about them even though they may have exhibited behavior that was less than desirable. Also, it would be a great time to praise the student, if they have been adhering to the advisory norms. This starts to reinvest currency back into the relationship piggy bank after the recent withdrawal.

ADVISORY IS SUPPORT

ENCOURAGING STUDENT GROWTH AND ACADEMIC SUCCESS

ACADEMIC PLANNING AND SUPPORT

In some cases advisory has become synonymous with study hall, when in reality it is so much more. What could be done to support students academically during advisory? Let's find out.

Preparing Students for Success

Many advisory periods focus solely on student growth and academic performance. However, the power of an advisor is to take this time and utilize it not just as a study hall but for teaching how to become a better student and a better person in the long run. Advisory, under these circumstances, should feel like a supportive and encouraging environment as young scholars work toward their academic goals. Many advisors will generally think that giving students the time to work on missing assignments is enough; however, challenge this assumption. In what ways can you take a more hands-on approach to empowering students to take control of their academics?

Study Skills

Modern research about the ineffectiveness of homework is creating an environment where homework is not valued by educators and, as an extension, students. As a result, students are not using time outside of class to study. Advisors can support the work of teachers by improving students' study habits. Advisory can be a place where students are taught note taking skills, how to study for upcoming assessments, as well as test taking strategies.

Time Management and Organization

Young people have a rare superpower. They have a gift that allows them to see deadlines far into the future even though they are already here! Time management and organization can help students reduce stress and have better grades. To get students started, consider having a calendaring session using digital calendaring tools. Additionally, students can organize their cloud and drive files with the support of an advisor. There are tons of resources available to support students in learning effective time management and organizational strategies. Below are a few apps that can help.

Apps for Time Management and Organization

Evernote

Google Calendar

Focus Booster

Trello

ACADEMIC PLANNING AND SUPPORT

One on one conversations about study skills, test taking strategies, or supporting teens emotionally who are having a rough time in school, are great ways to make this time purposeful.

Academic Planning

One guidance counselor usually serves over 100 students. It would be difficult for her/him/them to have deep and meaningful conversations with each student about academic plans. This is another area that an advisor can lend support. Because advisors know students' grades and personalities well, they can assist with choosing classes or electives that align with their specific interests. Additionally, they can answer questions and make sure students are aware of any remedial classes they need to take. Lastly, great advisors can make connections with the classes scholars are taking now and their future plans.

Monitoring Progress

Adolescents need a caring adult to not only check in on their academic progress but to regularly monitor and provide feedback on this progress. Advisors should design a system or procedure that has students regularly checking their grades, identifying academic skill gaps, and creating a plan for remediation. Usually schools have some type of online resource used for students to work on skill deficits. However, this leaves students a bit out of the accountability loop. Research has shown that when students are aware of their grades, they usually make improvements to do better. Monitoring student progress in advisory looks like having a serious discussion about where kids are academically and helping them to create a plan with actionable steps to progress toward making improvement.

Goal Setting

Setting goals, both short and long term help young people develop a sense of purpose and direction. However, goal setting does not come easy for teens. They need time to understand what is being asked of them and to practice writing goals that are SMART (specific, measure, attainable, realistic, and time-bound). Once young people have learned to set SMART goals they can confidently and strategically work on plans to meet both personal and academic milestones for success. Take a look at this lesson plan to support goal setting in your classroom.

ADVISORY LESSON PLAN: GOAL-DEN ROAD

This lesson is great to do near the end of a marking period. This activity has flexible timing (between 20–50 mins) with minimal planning/prep. if necessary you can break it into two mini lessons.

PURPOSE

Goal setting is something that is extremely difficult for those who have never sat down and given any thought about the future in a methodical way. This lesson is a great introduction to goal setting.

CASEL Competency/SEL Focus:
Building self management by setting personal goals

MATERIALS

Projector/Whiteboard
Laptops
Colored pencils/Markers
Yellow construction paper cut into large rectangles

ACTIVITY

Have students pair up and think about a goal, big or small, that they set for themselves and achieved. Have them share the experience with their partner. If they can't think of a goal that they achieved, have them talk about a challenge they faced and how they overcame. Have 2-3 students share out their experiences with the advisory. Inform students that today they are going to be talking about goal setting and how to use goal setting to help manage their lives. Divide students into groups and assign them each a letter from the SMART goal (specific, measurable, attainable, realistic, time bound). They will need to create a definition of the word as it relates to goals (can be looked up online for inspiration). It should be simple enough for a first grader to understand. Students must also jot down an example of a goal that is specific, measurable, attainable, relevant, or time bound to illustrate their definition. Students will present their definition and example to the rest of the class.

Ask the following probing questions as students present to help them deepen their understanding of the concepts:

- How do you know if your goal is too specific?
- How will that goal be measured?
- What do you need to know about …. to make this goal more attainable?
- Is this important to you? Why or why not?
- How long is too long to work on a goal?

ADVISORY LESSON PLAN: GOAL-DEN ROAD

This lesson is great to do near the end of a marking period. This activity has flexible timing (between 20–50 mins) with minimal planning/prep. if necessary you can break it into two mini lessons.

PURPOSE

Goal setting is something that is extremely difficult for those who have never sat down and given any thought about the future in a methodical way. This lesson is a great introduction to goal setting.

CASEL Competency/SEL Focus:
Building self management by setting personal goals

MATERIALS

Projector/Whiteboard
Laptops
Colored pencils/Markers
Yellow construction paper cut into large rectangles

ACTIVITY (CONT'D)

Have students return to their seats and review any misunderstandings with each other/and advisor. Inform students it is now time to work on your own SMART goal. This goal should be something that is relevant to them either academically or personally. Have students work independently or in pairs to draft their SMART Goals. They can take turns giving one another feedback on how to make the goal more specific, measurable, attainable, realistic, and time bound. When students have finished drafting their goal they will get a yellow rectangle and copy their goal to be posted on the Goal-den Road. Everyone will share their goal aloud with the advisory and explain how their goal is specific, measurable, attainable, realistic, and time bound. The goals will be posted in the advisory space to form a road. Students can reflect on their goal daily and help support one another to achieve.

DEBRIEF

- How will we hold each other accountable for our goals?
- What other goals do you have?
- How could you use this skill in the future?

ACADEMIC PLANNING AND SUPPORT

Academic planning advisory is a great place to discuss requirements for graduation, credits, and other academic situations to keep scholars informed.

SEL Skills for Success

As students are monitoring and improving their academic outcomes it will be essential to support them with SEL skills such as resilience, self-advocacy, and self reflection. Making teens self-aware and reflective helps create patterns of accountability that will serve them well in the future. These skills should be explicitly discussed and framed as qualities that will help them in school and in the real world. Consider building common language around these traits so scholars can point to specific areas of personal growth they need to become better students and better people.

Students have a spectrum of stories from amazing to horrible that recount their experiences in school. Advisors can help young people who don't traditionally "do school" well find success. By providing students a nurturing and supportive environment that fosters growth and academic accountability, harm can be undone. Students who once hated school can rekindle their love of learning.

WHERE DO I START?

Use these tips to get started with helping students with academic planning and growth

1. Set clear expectations for behavior, language, and communication during academic planning advisory. What should students be doing while you are speaking with someone individually? What are the expectations for communicating? What should students be working on/have prepared for their one on one meeting?
2. Create a schedule to have weekly checkins with students about grades.
3. Create an agenda for your one on one conversations with students. What will students be required to bring to the meeting? How should they prepare for the conversation? Students should have something that keeps them accountable and invested in this time.
4. Develop activities/lessons for a study skill (i.e. taking notes, scheduling study time, etc.) and an SEL competency that supports academic planning (i.e. grit, understanding learning styles, etc.)
5. Seek to understand students' previous experiences in school, both positive and negative. Identifying this will give you a heads up on scholars who have struggled in school before and will allow you to find specific ways to support.

Chapter
SIX

ADVISORY IS FAMILY

PARTNERING WITH FAMILIES AND COMMUNITY

PARTNERING WITH FAMILIES AND COMMUNITY

The skills that young people learn and practice during advisory are ones that can be utilized in the real world. Help them make these connections.

Researchers have documented the importance of family and community engagement in numerous studies. When families and communities are involved in schools, adolescents perform better academically, have improved attendance, and can readily see connections to their world. Parents and the surrounding community are often untapped resources in school. As you continue to make your advisory a stellar and impactful experience for students, consider the following to engage families and the community.

Host Student Led Conferences

A student-led conference is a meeting, usually between a student or group of students, their parents/guardians, and their advisor/teacher(s). The purpose of these conferences is to twofold: 1. Young people can present academic progress, detailing strengths and weaknesses, to their parents/guardians and 2. They can share personal goals and aspirations. With proper scaffolding and practice, the student takes charge of leading the discussion and sharing their work, which can include tests, essays, projects, or her/his/their report card. These conferences are generally focused on promoting student learning, self-reflection, accountability, and seek to build stronger connections between students, families, and teachers. The "A-ha moments" you live for as an educator come alive during student led conferences.

Here are a few examples for you to check out online

Middle School Student Led Conference
https://www.youtube.com/watch?v=R9y2kEGnMR4

High School Student Led Conference
https://www.youtube.com/watch?v=n5ec1qwGJHE

Celebrate Together

Consider planning a celebration and inviting families to participate. It is a great way for families to visit the school and have a positive experience. This could look like a Thanksgiving/Harvest Day Luncheon, a Holiday Karaoke Party, or an end of the year barbecue. If these are usually school wide functions, set yourself apart by getting custom shirts or having activities that only the families of your advisory members can participate.

PARTNERING WITH FAMILIES AND COMMUNITY

Building a relationship with parents is just as important as relationship building with students. Talk to them often and keep them informed.

Call Home with Good News

As a parent, calls from school usually fall into two categories: announcements/reminders and when a kid has done something wrong. Imagine being a parent that also had struggles in school. These interactions could be continuing an antagonistic relationship that started way before the child stepped into your classroom.

Advisors can do a lot to change this narrative. Make it a practice to call home with good news. Celebrate students progress and thank parents for the work they are doing on their end. Parents need to feel as though they are a valued member of the educational team and not just an unconscious observer. This starts with an open line of communication with someone that knows their child well, the advisor.

Service Learning Projects

Community service is a phenomenal way to connect with a local organization and gives students an opportunity to practice the skills they have been learning during advisory. But, if you mention community service to a group of young people, you may hear some low grumbles. However, once they dive into a service project, that apprehension usually turns to smiles and laughter. Service learning helps students understand civic responsibility by promoting empathy and pride in giving back to her/his/their community. If it is difficult to get off campus, invite community organizations to host service events at the school.

Internships/Mentorships/Job Shadowing

Connecting local business with students is the definition of a win-win. Students get rich real world experience and exposure; mentors get the opportunity to share their knowledge and in kind labor to help their businesses grow. Additionally, students will be confident and prepared when it is time to enter the job market. Their resume will have valuable experience that could set them apart when job searching and on college applications.

School Partnerships

Bridging the gap from middle school to high school and high school to college can be a struggle for students and families. By having other school partners on the next level, students can know firsthand what it takes to be successful once they graduate and move on. Invite speakers from your partner schools, host application & informational events, or go on a tour so students can get immersed in the school they will be moving on to after they graduate.

FAMILY & COMMUNITY PARTNERSHIPS

WHERE DO I START?

It may seem like a heavy lift with a lot of planning to make this happen. Don't feel overwhelmed! Connecting your advisory with families and community doesn't have to be difficult. Here are a few ideas to get you started.

START

1. TAP YOUR PERSONAL NETWORK

Your personal network is usually a great place to start when connecting to community members. Often they can suggest resources or become a resource themselves. Think about scheduling people you know to come and speak to your advisory about their passions, interests, or skills necessary to be successful in life.

2. RESEARCH PREVIOUS PARTNERSHIPS

Ask veteran teachers and administrators if they have any contacts from community partners that aren't with the school anymore. Often the organization would love to partner with the school again but for one or another reason they cannot (i.e. teacher contact left, program contact changed, program temporarily lost funding, etc.). Reach out and see if a new connection can be established.

3. SURVEY PARENTS ABOUT THEIR NEEDS

Schools are places that should make servicing students and families top priority. Talk to parents and find out their pain points. Where could they use support or resources to help their child? Once you have a list of these needs loop in administration or other stakeholders to work on filling those gaps.

4. INVOLVE STUDENTS

After some practice and preparation, have students make a list of companies in their area and reach out to them directly. They could reach out to secure a guest speaker, ask them questions about their career, or get donations for a school project.

4. CALL PARENTS

Call parents of ALL students in your advisory and introduce yourself and your role as advisor within the first two weeks of school. Invite parents to a school event or tell them about a positive experience you had with their child.

SUCCESS

ADVISORY IS GROWTH
CONTINUOUS REFLECTION AND IMPROVEMENT

Getting students to reflect promotes self awareness and honesty.
A healthy culture of reflection makes it easy for students
to give one another critical feedback.

Getting Students to be Honest About Themselves

Having students reflect is a powerful tool. It is another instance when advisors see the a-ha spark light up in their students' eyes. Advisory should offer ample opportunities for students to reflect on their personal and academic development. Here are a few ways that it can be done in your advisory.

Journaling

Encourage students to keep a personal learning journal where they reflect on what they learned, how they learned it, and what lessons they might take away from their experiences. This could be embedded in the advisory schedule either weekly or daily. Journaling is a great practice to have students share personal thoughts with you as well. As an added method of feedback, think about writing back to your students in their journals.

Presentations of Learning

Authentic methods of assessment can be a bit of a challenge in schools. However, presentations of learning offer the student an opportunity to showcase their growth and development in an authentic way. Students prepare a presentation to showcase work they are proud of, their academic strengths and weaknesses, and what personal character traits they have been building through social and emotional learning. The work can be presented to their advisory, parents, or other trusted adult.

One on Ones

Insightful conversations with students about their growth are common when they speak with advisors one on one. This looks like all students working on an activity independently while you speak with an individual student. One on Ones also assist in building trust with students. Students aren't distracted and the private nature of the conversation allows the student to be honest with their advisor and with themselves.

Portfolio

Portfolios are a great way for students to visually see the progress they have been making. If they have an essay that they have worked on and revised, all of the drafts would be artifacts to include in their portfolio. They see each time they worked on it, the piece of writing got better. Students have access to specific targets and objectives to refer to. With a glimpse, they are able to make connections with where they are struggling and succeeding academically.

ONE ON ONE MEETING AGENDA

This One on One meeting agenda can be adapted for your specific advisory's structure by tailoring the work progress section to meet your needs. If you have a large advisory, consider meeting with up to 3 students at a time.

GENERAL CHECKIN (5 MINS)

HOW ARE YOU?

Use this time to check in with students. Ask if they have anything they would like to share from their world or see how they feel about the upcoming meeting. At times this checkin can take the duration of the meeting. Be sure to allow space for the student to share while gently moving the discussion forward.

MATERIAL CHECK (5 MINS)

CAN I SEE YOUR...?

Students should have specific materials that they bring to the one on one meeting to be prepared to discuss his/her/their progress. You might require students to bring a laptop with their Google calendar, current grades/ progress reports, their portfolio, or assignments that they are struggling to complete. This step adds another level of accountability for the one on one meeting.

WORK PROGRESS (15 MINS)

HOW CAN I HELP?

During the work progress section you are assisting the young person with a specific task geared toward helping her/him/them grow. This could look like reviewing revisions, helping with a difficult assignment, getting organized, or giving feedback. The expectations for what will be worked on should be guided by the student. Action plans and next steps should be agreed upon before the meeting is closed.

NEXT STEPS (5 MINS)

WHAT'S NEXT?

Students should leave the meeting with 1-2 next steps they can work on after the meeting. A plan should be discussed detailing follow up. Be sure to check back in with the student before their next meeting to see if the next steps were completed.

SELF REFLECTION

We can't expect students to do something that we are not willing to do ourselves. Take the time to make sure that you are modeling the social emotional intelligence and vulnerability that you are teaching your advisory.

Being Honest With Yourself

Self-reflection is the backbone of advisory. It enables you to identify areas for improvement and strengthen the experience for the members of your advisory in the future. In education, it is commonplace to put your own emotional safety and well being to the side quite often. As an advisor, that is not wise and this behavior must be recognized but not normalized. You need to be honest and evaluate your own social emotional capacity. How can we teach students how to work well in groups if it is something we struggle with personally? Be honest with students about your own progress and growth as an advisor, and when you are ready, as a person. It helps to build trust and show students that this is what lifelong learning looks like.

Check in With Yourself

Educators who care are their own worst critics. You beat yourself up and go down rabbit holes of "shoulda, coulda, woulda". It's ok to analyze your effectiveness as an advisor. But before you do that, check in with your own social emotional growth and development. If you are to teach students SEL, it's crucial that you become a learner as well and continue your own SEL development to show up as your best self for young people. As you examine yourself, use the prompts below to help spark an honest assessment. After you've looked at all of the things that could have been better in advisory, be sure to celebrate your wins. Students will start showing many changes once advisory is in full swing. Next, give yourself some grace and space. Everything that was made well took time to build. Learning is a process. So is teaching. Forgive others, forgive yourself and focus on the positive. Give some love to yourself for the important work that you do. You deserve it.

Self Care

This MUST be in your teacher toolkit from Day 1. Self care comes in many shapes and forms. Waking up early to be the only one seeing the sun, a weekly manicure with your cell phone on silent, or taking care of your garden; everyone has a different way to decompress. As an advisor the work can get heavy. In those moments we have to take time to make sure we are ok. Scheduling self care makes it a priority. Create a self care plan with specific directions for when you are triggered or need a reset from a difficult situation. Set timers and reminders to check in with yourself and to do something that makes your soul happy.

SELF REFLECTION QUESTIONS

1. How have I grown as a person from your experiences in advisory?
2. What new skills have I learned that can help I... As a teacher? As a parent? As a coworker? In some other capacity?
3. What SEL weaknesses do you have that I would like to work on?
4. In what ways can I address these weaknesses when I am ready?
5. Am I ok? How do I know?

SELF CARE PLAN

AFFIRMATIONS FOR SUCCESS

1. _____
2. _____
3. _____

SELF CARE APPOINTMENTS

DATE & TIME	ACTIVITY

GOALS/PURPOSE

_____
_____
_____
_____

NAME:
....

WHEN I AM TRIGGERED I CAN

_____
_____
_____
_____

WHEN I NEED HELP I'LL REACH OUT TO

DAILY DE-STRESS ACTIVITIES

NOTES

GROWING AS AN ADVISOR

Advisory is dynamic and should change to meet the needs of students. Check in with students periodically to ensure advisory is meeting their needs.

Get Student Feedback

Advisory only works well if it is working for students. Getting real time feedback on advisory activities will give you specific data for ideas about how to revise lessons, activities, or debriefing questions. Student feedback can be given informally with a quick exit ticket or focus group. If you are looking for a more formal method, consider a survey or analyzing school information system data points (attendance, behavior referrals, etc.).

Collaboration

Your advisory is your own; however, a sense of collaboration among advisors is a great way to share resources to cut planning time in half. Also, working together can give you insight into what activities or lessons worked well and which ones need to be tweaked. Collaborating with other advisors also gives advisory a friendly sense of competition and comradery. Problems that arise can be shared among the group and workshopped to generate a solution that will benefit all.

Fill Your Toolbox

To most educators, advisory is a fairly new experience. More and more educator training programs mention SEL and advisory but targeted professional development in this area is lacking. There is lot of information on the internet about advisory and how to do it effectively. It may seem overwhelming, but it is imperative to fill your tool box, one tool at a time. Digest resources slowly over time and implement them incrementally. In advisory, less is more. Build a foundation of trust with students and let other opportunities blossom. Every tool doesn't work for every advisor, and that's ok. Advisory is what you make it. Don't be afraid to pivot when a particular strategy or activity isn't successful.

SELF REFLECTION QUESTIONS

1. What Social Emotional learning topics were easy to teach? Which ones did you struggle with?
2. What are your Top 5 Moments in Advisory? What successes can I celebrate?
3. Evaluate your relationship with each student in your advisory. Who do I know well? Who am I struggling to connect with?
4. What weaknesses do I have that I'd like to work on?
5. What new activities, suggestions would I like to incorporate moving forward?
6. Have my students made progress both personally and academically? How do I know?

See an Awesome Advisory in Action

To help reflect on your practice, check out a high functioning advisory in action. Setting up time to visit a classroom will enable you to see the suggestions and theory behind advisory come to life. If your schedule doesn't allow, videos on Youtube are a great place to start. As you watch consider the following questions to help you unpack the observation:

1. What do student to student interactions look like?
2. What do advisor to student interactions look like?
3. How does the advisory communicate?
4. Where is there evidence of students knowing each other well?
5. Where is there evidence of students' connection to their advisor?
6. What inspiration can you gain from the physical space?
7. What SEL skills are on display?
8. What activities are being featured?
9. How is advisory learning debriefed?
10. What ideas would you like to implement?

Great Advisories in Action

Nashville Big Picture School	https://www.youtube.com/watch?v=KF06hmf6XEA
Springfield Renaissance School	https://www.youtube.com/watch?v=sLXFuuUpj1U
A Different Look at Advisory	https://www.youtube.com/watch?v=Nu_1BWSAOJI
The Met Big Picture High School	https://www.youtube.com/watch?v=TdEyugnWf6w

WHERE DO I START?

Use these tips to get started establishing a culture of reflection

1. Complete your self care plan. Schedule self care 2-3 times per week and follow through!
2. Decide how you will support student reflection. Choose a format (journaling, presentations of learning, etc.) and develop a schedule to implement. Take time to decide how you will model and share these expectations with students.
3. Make sure students know how to access their grades and attendance data.
4. Create your first week one on one schedule. How often will you meet with students and for how long?
5. Create a one on one agenda. Be sure to review the expectations of one on one meetings with your advisory.

NOW YOU KNOW

Congratulations! You have taken an important step toward creating a successful advisory program. There is a lot to digest in this workbook. However, implementing these practices and strategies are just the start of the journey. It is my hope that you now know the answer to the question "What is advisory?". Along with it, I also hope you gained valuable insight and strategies to build strong relationships that support students in this critical phase of their lives. Advisory is not just another period in the school day but an opportunity to connect with students on a much deeper level, to help them navigate challenges, and to inspire them to reach their full potential.

As we face increasingly complex and uncertain times, the need for advisory becomes even more urgent. Students today are dealing with a range of issues, from social media anxiety to academic pressure and mental health concerns. These crises require a holistic and compassionate approach. Advisory becomes that place where young people can find a listening ear and a kind word.

Advisory is not just for students. It is also a platform for educators to connect with their peers, to collaborate on best practices, and to develop their own social emotional competencies. As you support your students, you also need to take care of yourself and cultivate a culture of wellness and growth.

Advisory can be so many things. Whether it is helping a student overcome a personal challenge, fostering a sense of belonging in a diverse community, or igniting a spark of curiosity and creativity; advisory is a catalyst for growth and transformation. Making advisory truly impactful is a journey. Trust me, it doesn't just happen overnight. Take initiative and think beyond the classroom walls and engage with families, community members, and other stakeholders to make sure the time and space for advisory is protected and valued.

Now, it's time for action. Let's take action to create more opportunities in advisory to learn from one another, innovate, and adapt to the changing needs of our students in our world. Let's celebrate the successes and the challenges advisory holds, acknowledging that it is a dynamic and ever evolving practice that requires courage, dedication, and resilience. Let's embrace the joys of working with young people, the sense of purpose and fulfillment that comes with making a difference in their lives. Let's create a better future for our students. They deserve it.

REFERENCES & RESOURCES

Ani, A. (2013). In Spite of Racism, Inequality, and School Failure: Defining Hope with Achieving Black Children. Journal of Negro Education, 82, 408 - 421.

Boyes-Watson, C. and Pranis, K. (2015) Circle Forward: Building a Restorative School Community. Living Justice Press, St. Paul.

Davenport, M. (2018). Using Circle Practice in the Classroom. Edutopia. https://www.edutopia.org/article/using-circle-practice-classroom/

EL Education. (2018, January 19). High School Student-Led Conference [Video]. YouTube. https://www.youtube.com/watch?v=n5ec1qwGJHE

Galloway, M. K., Conner, J., & Pope, D. (2013). Nonacademic Effects of Homework in Privileged, High-Performing High Schools. Journal of Experimental Education, 81(4), 490–510. https://doi.org/10.1080/00220973.2012.745469

Hale, M. (2022, April 6). Top Benefits of Family and Community Engagement | Hanover Research. Hanover Research. https://www.hanoverresearch.com/insights-blog/top-benefits-of-family-and-community-engagement/?org=k-12-education

Harmony SEL. (2021, October 15). Social Emotional Learning (SEL) Program, Activities & Curriculum - Harmony. Harmony. https://www.harmonysel.org/

International Institute for Restorative Practices (2018) Restoring Community. https://www.iirp.edu/defining-restorative/5-2-circles

Key Lessons: What Research Says About the Value of Homework. (2013, November 12). Reading Rockets. https://www.readingrockets.org/article/key-lessons-what-research-says-about-value-homework

Littky, D., & Grabelle, S. (2012). The Big Picture: Education Is Everyone's Business. ASCD.

Murphy, J. & Decker, K. (2014). The effects of grades, achievement, and performance feedback on motivation. Journal of Educational Psychology, 106(3), 764-775

Rācene, A. (2017). Importance of Goal-Setting Tasks in Career Counseling.

Raise the Bar Parents. (2014, January 30). Student Led Parent Teacher Conference - Middle School [Video]. YouTube. https://www.youtube.com/watch?v=R9y2kEGnMR4

Robinson, K., & Aronica, L. (2016). Creative Schools: The Grassroots Revolution That's Transforming Education. Penguin Books.

Social and Emotional Learning | CASEL - Casel Schoolguide. (n.d.). https://schoolguide.casel.org/

Sedlacek, W. (2017). Measuring Noncognitive Variables: Improving Admissions, Success and Retention for Underrepresented Students. Stylus Publishing, LLC.

NOTES

NOTES

NOTES

NOTES

NOTES

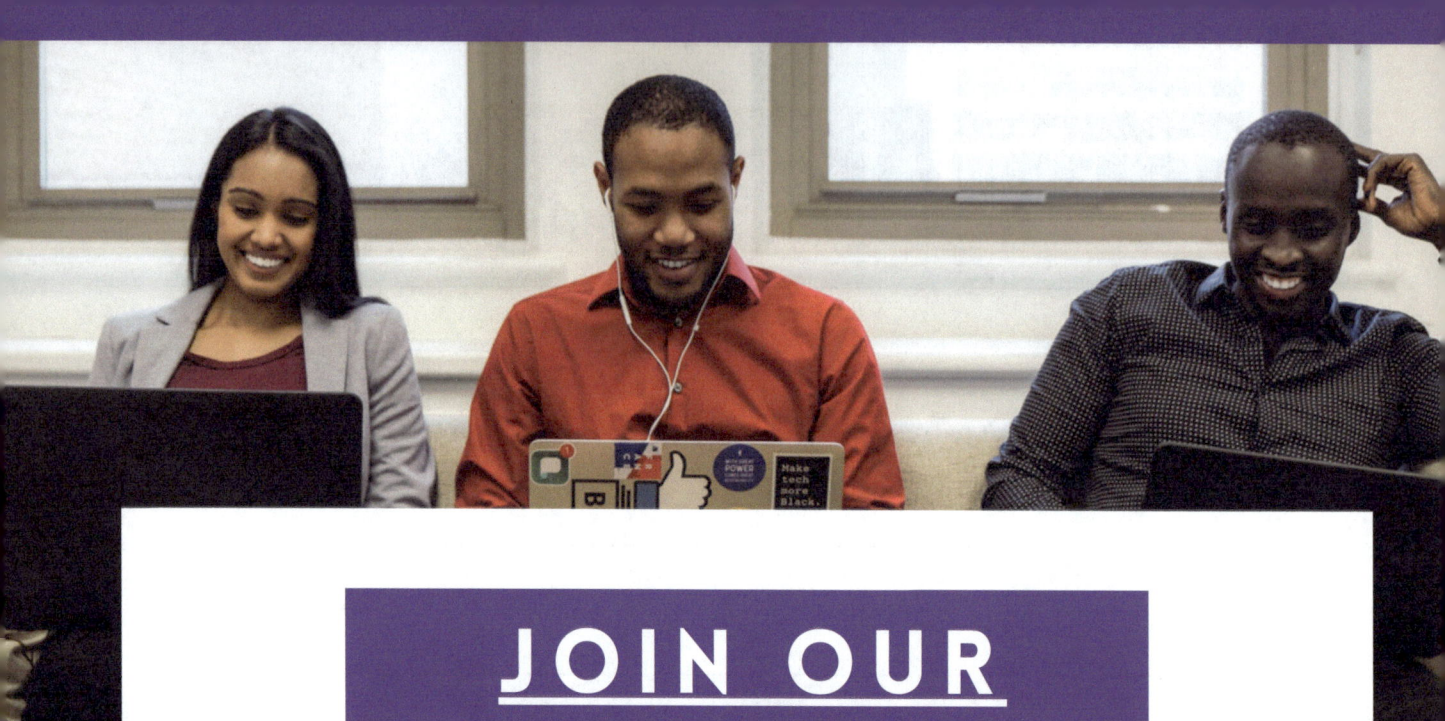

JOIN OUR MAILING LIST!

ARE YOU READY TO TRULY CHAMPION SOCIAL EMOTIONAL LEARNING AT YOUR SCHOOL?

The SEL Champion Mailing List will be a great resource for all of your SEL classroom integration needs. To get exclusive access to SEL tips, strategies, and discount codes on upcoming online courses, sign up today! Follow @Bwitcher_SELChampion on Instagram & Facebook for more details!

SIGN UP TODAY!

SEL CHAMPIONS COURSE

TEACHERS NEW TO SOCIAL AND EMOTIONAL LEARNING,
YOU DON'T WANT TO MISS THIS!!!!

BRAND NEW ONLINE COURSE

SEL Champion

WITH BRANDON WITCHER

SIGN UP NOW

FOLLOW @BWITCHER_SELCHAMPION ON INSTAGRAM & FACEBOOK FOR MORE DETAILS!

SOCIAL EMOTIONAL LEARNING IS MORE THAN JUST A CHECK-IN

ABOUT THE AUTHOR
BRANDON WITCHER

Brandon Witcher is an educator, writer, consultant, and social emotional learning expert with over fifteen years experience in urban education. He has taught all grade levels and continues to be a staunch advocate of social emotional learning and project based learning; particularly for its benefits for young people who are traditionally underserved. He has consulted with teachers and school/district leaders all over America, discussing topics such as teaching young men of color, advisory practices, project based learning, and strategic integration of social emotional learning. He holds a Bachelor's degree from The Lincoln University in English and a Master's of Education from Wilmington University. He enjoys eating at vegan restaurants, singing at the top of mountains after a good hike, and advocating for educational change for young people.

BWITCHER_SELCHAMPION

BWITCHER_SELCHAMPION

SELCHAMPIONLEARNING@GMAIL.COM

LEAVE A
REVIEW

I hope you enjoyed this workbook and found lots of value to help you and your students! I would appreciate if you wouldn't mind taking the time to leave a review on Amazon. Thanks!

Brandon Witcher

Made in United States
Troutdale, OR
06/02/2024

20262486R00042